MEDICAL
Inventions
THE BEST OF HEALTH

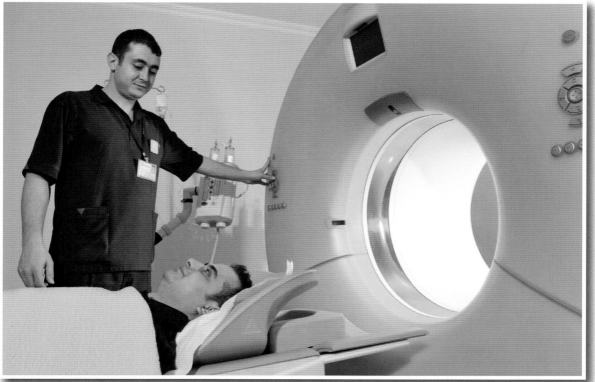

Jill Bryant

Crabtree Publishing Company
www.crabtreebooks.com

INVENTIONS THAT SHAPED THE MODERN WORLD

Author: Jill Bryant
Publishing plan research and development:
  Reagan Miller
Editors: James Gladstone, Rachel Eagen
Copy editor: Dimitra Chronopoulos
Proofreader: Janice Dyer
Editorial services: Clarity Content Services
Design: Pixel Hive Studio
Cover design: Samara Parent
Photo research: Linda Tanaka
Project coordinator and prepress technician:
  Samara Parent
Print coordinator: Margaret Amy Salter
Series consultants:
Professor D. Eric Walters, Ph.D.
  Rosalind Franklin University of Medicine and Science
Jane Hutchison, Masters of Education

Front cover: a doctor using an old x-ray machine on a patient's chest (left); a patient entering a Magnetic Resonance Imaging (MRI) machine (right)
Back cover: a sphygmomanometer, or blood pressure meter

Photographs: front cover right iStock/Thinkstock, left Everett Collection/shutterstock, back cover fotohunter/shutterstock, p1 Levent Konuk/shutterstock, p4 Jerzy Strzelecki/CCL; p6 U.S. National Library of Medicine; p7 yang na/shutterstock; p9 wavebreakmedia/shutterstock; p10 U.S. National Library of Medicine; p11 Bettmann/ CORBIS; p12 U.S. National Library of Medicine; p13 Institut Pasteur; p14 left U.S. National Library of Medicine, Rama/CCL; p16 U.S. National Library of Medicine; p17 Photo courtesy of thinklabsmedical.com; p18–19 Thackray Museum, Jupiterimages/Thinkstock; p20 Photo courtesy of crtsite.com; p21 U.S. National Library of Medicine; p22 Wellcome Library, London; p23 U.S. National Library of Medicine; p25 Michael Anderson/National Cancer Institute; p26 Philipcosson/CCL; p27 Corbin O'Grady Studio/Science Photo Library; p28 marilyn barbone/shutterstock; p29 Science Photo Library; p30 U.S. National Library of Medicine; p31 Photo courtesy of Harvard University; p32 U.S. National Library of Medicine; p34 Wellcome Images; p36 iStockphoto/Thinkstock; p37 U.S. National Library of Medicine, National Institute of Health; p38 U.S. National Library of Medicine; p39 Mayovskyy Andrew/shutterstock; p40 left Lynn Johnson/National Geographic Creative, Image courtesy Össur, Inc.; p42 Photo courtesy of Dr. Mehran Anvari, Centre for Surgical Invention & Innovation (CSii).

Library and Archives Canada Cataloguing in Publication

Bryant, Jill, author
    Medical inventions : the best of health / Jill Bryant.

(Inventions that shaped the modern world)
Includes index.
Issued in print and electronic formats.
ISBN 978-0-7787-0212-2 (bound).--ISBN 978-0-7787-0232-0 (pbk.).--
ISBN 978-1-4271-9423-7 (pdf).--ISBN 978-1-4271-9419-0 (html)

    1. Medical innovations--Juvenile literature. I. Title.

RA418.5.M4B79 2013   j610   C2013-906244-0
                                          C2013-906245-9

Library of Congress Cataloging-in-Publication Data

Bryant, Jill, author.
    Medical inventions : the best of health / Jill Bryant.
        pages cm. -- (Inventions that shaped the modern world)
    Audience: 10-13.
    Audience: Grades 4-6.
    Includes index.
    ISBN 978-0-7787-0212-2 (reinforced library binding : alk. paper) -- ISBN 978-0-7787-0232-0 (pbk. : alk. paper) -- ISBN 978-1-4271-9423-7 (electronic pdf : alk. paper) -- ISBN 978-1-4271-9419-0 (electronic html : alk. paper)
    1. Medicine--History--Juvenile literature. 2. Medical innovations--History--Juvenile literature. 3. Medical technology--Juvenile literature. I. Title.

R133.5.B797 2014
610--dc23

                                          2013036067

Crabtree Publishing Company

www.crabtreebooks.com   1-800-387-7650

Printed in Canada/102013/BF20130920

Published in Canada
Crabtree Publishing
616 Welland Ave.
St. Catharines, ON
L2M 5V6

Published in the United States
Crabtree Publishing
PMB 59051
350 Fifth Avenue, 59th Floor
New York, New York 10118

Published in the United Kingdom
Crabtree Publishing
Maritime House
Basin Road North, Hove
BN41 1WR

Published in Australia
Crabtree Publishing
3 Charles Street
Coburg North
VIC, 3058

Contents

Ancient Healers

Sick? Injured? Need a healing hand? Back in the ancient world, people became ill and injured themselves in many of the same ways we do today. Learned healers helped the sick and injured long before the age of hospitals and medical schools. These healers from the past were medical inventors and innovators. Without the contribution of these men and women, we would not be able to treat and cure as many illnesses as we can today. We owe a lot to our ancestors.

In ancient Babylonia—modern-day Iran and Iraq—some priests worked as healers. They noted **symptoms** and consulted clay tablets that outlined the treatment for different illnesses.

↑ *This is Tutankhamun's death mask. In life, ancient Egyptian pharaohs wore green eye makeup containing copper salts, which had antiseptic, healing properties. This eye shadow helped to treat eye **infections**.*

Medicines made from plants and minerals, in forms such as pills, **salves**, vapors, and **balms**, were used to treat coughs, headaches, fevers, and other ailments.

Ancient Egyptian doctors applied pressure to stop the flow of blood from bleeding wounds. This technique is now used by health care professionals all over the world today.

Ancient Egyptian healers used herbs, other plants, and minerals to make medicines. They also made early forms of cough drops and mouthwash. These remedies helped to relieve sore throats and bad coughs.

The ancient Egyptians understood the basics of breathing and **circulation**.

They knew that people draw in air through their noses. They also knew that the heart was central to the human body. They thought the rhythmic pulsing of the heart made the air flow to the heart and to other parts of the body.

Agnodice
Building on the Work of female healers

Agnodice was a female doctor who is said to have lived in ancient Greece in the fourth century BCE. Little is known about her life, but it is thought that she studied medicine in the city of Alexandria, Egypt. Agnodice cut her hair short and disguised herself as a man. This allowed her to practice medicine in the city of Athens. According to legend, when Agnodice revealed that she was a woman, the people were outraged, and she was put on trial. Agnodice's female patients defended Agnodice and her skills as a doctor. Ultimately, the law was changed so that women could practice medicine in ancient Athens.

↑ *Is the ancient Greek legend of Agnodice, the healer, fact or fiction?*

Healers of Ancient China

Ancient Chinese healers used sets of needles inserted into the skin to treat health problems. This practice is known as acupuncture and is still used today. It is now thought that acupuncture signals the brain to release chemicals in the body to reduce pain and **inflammation**.

These healers used hundreds of different plants in their medicines. For example, mulberry wood relieved pain and controlled high blood pressure. Chinese yams were used to stimulate appetite and treat fatigue.

Huang Ti (circa 2600 BCE), the father of Chinese medicine, believed that "the superior physician helps before the early budding of disease." In other words, a good physician guides patients to take good care of their health to avoid getting sick in the first place. This can mean eating healthy foods, exercising, and avoiding substances that are bad for the body, such as sugar.

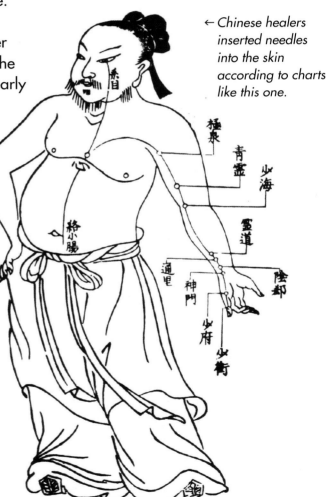

← Chinese healers inserted needles into the skin according to charts like this one.

"Delicious dishes banish tablets and pills, Nourishing food is the drug for all ills."

— no date

→ Foods such as ginger, fennel, walnuts, tea leaves, lotus seeds, dandelions, and scallions are used in Chinese herbal medicine.

Inventors, Inventions, and Innovations

Past and present medical inventors share many traits: curiosity, intelligence, and determination. They solve problems in creative ways. In this book, you'll learn about the invention of an antiseptic spray used to keep wounds clean during surgery. You'll learn about the invention of the stethoscope. You'll also explore inventions that help people with physical challenges to move faster.

But what is an invention? What is an innovation? What is a discovery?

- An invention is a new product or the introduction of a new process. A stethoscope is an invention that allows a doctor to listen to a person's heart.
- An innovation is when someone improves or makes a major contribution to an existing product or process. An ear thermometer is an

example of an innovation because it allows body temperature to be taken through the ear, rather than under the tongue, which many people find unpleasant.

- A discovery is something that is found, or revealed, for the first time—for example, the discovery of **insulin** to treat diabetes.

There are also incredible technologies in the field of medicine. A medical technology is a tool or device used to identify health problems. An X-ray is an example of a medical technology. It shows a doctor if a bone is broken.

Many inventions build upon previous ideas and technologies. They are constantly evolving to improve the health of people young and old.

CHAPTER ONE

Sanitation

Germs Spread Disease

"Wash your hands," says your dad as you race to the dinner table. You groan, head to the bathroom, and reach for the soap. Today we understand the importance of washing hands to kill germs. But long ago, this wasn't the case.

↑ *By insisting on hand disinfection, Ignaz Semmelweis decreased the risk of death in the maternity ward where he studied to just two percent.*

In the Middle Ages, people thought dirt poisoned the air and bred disease. Millions of people died at the hands of the Black Death, an epidemic of bubonic plague, which struck Europe from 1348 to 1350. The King of England ordered his subjects to clean up the streets and dispose of rat-infested garbage. But cleaning the streets didn't solve the problem, and people continued to suffer.

Hand Washing

Centuries later, a Hungarian doctor named Ignaz Semmelweis (1818–1865) made an important discovery. Working in a Viennese hospital in the 1840s, Semmelweis saw that many new mothers died shortly after giving birth. Some women even preferred to give birth on the street to avoid the hospital, which was nicknamed a "death trap."

The maternity ward was next to a room where doctors conducted **autopsies**. Semmelweis noticed that doctors worked in both of these rooms. The doctors carried out medical procedures on new mothers and autopsies on dead bodies.

↑ *Today, doctors wash and scrub their hands with a disinfecting soap before and after performing surgeries. They also change their gowns before treating new patients.*

Simple changes in **sanitation** made a huge difference. Semmelweis told doctors and nurses to clean their hands by using a **disinfectant** called chlorinated lime. He also instructed staff to scrub the ward with **calcium chloride**. The number of deaths in the hospital dropped significantly. Semmelweis realized that his discovery might save the lives of thousands of women.

Semmelweis's ideas about hand hygiene were rejected by doctors in Vienna. Semmelweis returned to Budapest to continue his work. It took 20 years before his discoveries were accepted by other health care professionals. Today, hand washing and proper sanitation are extremely important in hospitals around the world.

Antiseptic Surgery

Louis Pasteur (1822–1895) was a French doctor who discovered that tiny organisms, which he called germs, made alcohol turn sour. Based on this finding, in 1862 he invented **pasteurization**. This process involved boiling and cooling a liquid to kill germs and harmful **bacteria** that can make people sick. Soon after Pasteur's discovery, milk was commonly pasteurized to make it safe for people to drink. Pasteur's work helped to support the germ theory that states microorganisms (germs, such as particular bacteria or viruses) cause disease in humans.

Joseph Lister

Joseph Lister (1827–1912) was inspired by the work of Louis Pasteur. In the 1860s, Lister applied Pasteur's findings about bacteria to make improvements in sanitation. Lister focused on the high number of patients who died while recovering from surgery. His idea was to clean patients' wounds with carbolic

Florence Nightingale

Building on the Work of Ignaz Semmelweis

British nurse Florence Nightingale (1820–1910) was famous for her work as a nurse during the Crimean War between the Russian Empire and England, France, and Sardinia. It lasted from March 1853 to April 1856 and was fought mostly on the Crimean peninsula in the Black Sea. Nightingale was a passionate advocate for hand washing. She encouraged cleanliness and proper sanitation in hospitals to prevent the deaths of soldiers. She saved countless lives that otherwise may have been lost from improper hygiene.

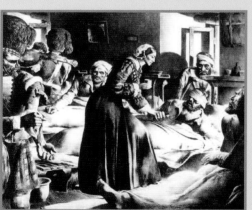

↑ Many health care workers during Florence Nightingale's time thought the poor didn't deserve medical care. Nightingale worked against this attitude. She made sure common soldiers received the medical care they needed.

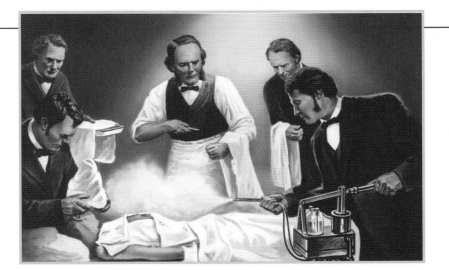

→ Lister invented an antiseptic spray to keep wounds clean during surgery. He was called the father of modern surgery for establishing sterile techniques in operating rooms.

acid, a strong disinfectant. Lister also soaked dressings in an antiseptic **solution**. These measures caused the death rate in hospitals to plunge. Others followed Lister's treatment regime, and this new technique saved lives and protected patients' health.

Lister wrote a letter to Louis Pasteur in 1874, thanking him for his discoveries. Without Pasteur's findings, Lister may not have developed his own ideas for sanitation.

Joseph Lister describes the effects of carbolic acid on raw sewage:

"In the course of the year 1864 I was much struck with an account of the remarkable effects produced by carbolic acid upon the sewage of the town of Carlisle, the admixture of a very small proportion not only preventing all odor from the lands irrigated with the refuse material, but, as it was stated, destroying the entozoa which usually infest cattle fed upon such pastures."

— Joseph Lister, 1867

Listerine was the first over-the-counter mouthwash, first available in 1914. It is named after Joseph Lister.

→ *While living in Turkey, Mary Wortley Montagu had her son inoculated against smallpox. On returning to England in 1722, she had her four-year-old daughter inoculated in front of the royal court. This encouraged Europeans to use this method to protect against smallpox.*

Vaccine Technologies

In medieval times, people knew they couldn't catch **smallpox** twice. They either died from it or developed **immunity** to it. People from Africa, India, and China used a method called **inoculation** to protect themselves. Doctors and healers took pus from a smallpox sore, then injected the pus into a cut on the arm or leg of a healthy person. The exposure to a small dose of smallpox allowed healthy people to develop an immunity against it.

Much later, in 1776, British soldiers in the New World, the lands of the Americas where the first Europeans arrived, stayed healthy during a smallpox outbreak. They had been inoculated against the disease. The healthy soldiers successfully defended Quebec in battle. George Washington made sure his American soldiers were inoculated after this military defeat.

Edward Jenner

Edward Jenner (1749–1823) had heard the rumors: dairymaids who caught a disease from cows called cowpox were strangely protected against smallpox.

In the late 1800s, German doctor Robert Koch (1843–1910) proved—without a doubt—that germs cause disease. His work helped pave the way for the development of modern **vaccines**.

Jenner **hypothesized** that cowpox protected people from smallpox. He inoculated a boy named James using pus from a dairymaid's cowpox **lesions**. The boy became feverish, but recovered. Jenner then inoculated James with smallpox. This time, James didn't react. He was protected! Jenner called the process vaccination. By the 1800s, Jenner's method became common practice through most of Europe.

In the last hundred years, vaccines have saved millions of lives around the world. Today, most children receive vaccines that protect them from serious illnesses such as polio, measles, mumps, and rubella.

In a scholarly paper about his vaccination process, Edward Jenner wrote:

"...but what renders the Cow Pox virus so extremely singular, is that the person who has been thus affected is for ever after secure from the infection of the Small Pox...."

— Edward Jenner, 1798

↓ *In 1900, Belgian doctor Jules Bordet (1870–1961) discovered the bacterium that causes **whooping cough**. This discovery eventually led to a vaccine for this disease, which has saved thousands of lives. Bordet was awarded the Nobel Prize in Physiology or Medicine in 1919.*

CHAPTER TWO

Medical Instruments

Health care workers use tools, or medical instruments, in their work. Doctors and nurses use medical instruments to check vital signs such as body temperature and blood pressure. Other instruments include scalpels for surgery and syringes to give medicine.

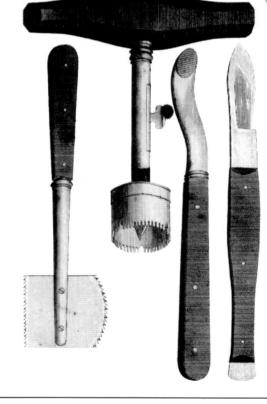

↑ A human skull, dating back 5000 years, shows where a trepanning tool made a large hole. For thousands of years, people believed this extreme treatment had positive health benefits.

One medical tool of the past was called a trephine. It was used for trepanning, a technique that involved drilling holes in the human skull.

← The tool with the round blade is a trephine.

Syringe

Ammar ibn Ali al-Mawsili (circa 1000 CE) was an Egyptian surgeon. He used a device like a syringe to remove cataracts, which are cloudy lenses that cover people's eyes. This syringe-like device drew the cloudy liquid cataract into a tube. But the device did not inject fluids.

Scottish doctor Alexander Wood (1817–1884) invented the syringe in 1853. This invention had a huge impact on the field of medicine. A syringe is a device that contains medicine and has a hollow needle tip. The needle tip pierces the skin so that medicine can be injected into a patient's bloodstream. Syringes can also be used in reverse to draw blood or other fluids out of a patient's body.

Wood's first syringe had a tube with a plunger that fit inside. He used it to inject a drug called morphine into patients for pain relief. Later, the tube and other parts were made of plastic. The devices were used widely by the end of the 1800s.

Syringes were **sterilized** and reused until the 1950s. This ensured they were safe, clean, and not carrying bacteria when they were used with a new patient.

In 1956, New Zealand pharmacist Colin Murdoch (1929–2008) developed the disposable syringe. This innovation offered greater safety and less risk of infection. The downside of disposable syringes is that they create **biohazardous** waste. This isn't good for the environment.

Murdoch's invention of the disposable syringe was prompted by a deep concern for fellow humans. During an interview, he said:

"Dangerous bacteria and viruses were transferred from one patient to another by doctors who used improperly sterilized reusable glass hypodermic syringes and needles to inject other patients."

— Colin Murdoch, 1993

Stethoscope

René-Théophile-Hyacinthe Laënnec (1781–1826) invented the stethoscope in Paris, France, in 1816. Before this invention, he and other doctors leaned over a patient, resting their ear directly on the patient's chest. This allowed doctors to hear the heartbeat. But this physical closeness sometimes made patients and doctors feel uncomfortable.

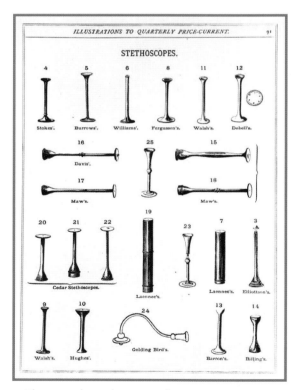

↑ These early stethoscope designs are not arranged in the order in which they were invented. Laënnec's—the first designs—are numbers 7 and 19.

Laënnec thought about how sound can be amplified over distance. He recalled seeing two children play with a plank of wood: one child used a pen to scratch one end of the plank, while the second child listened to the sound at the other end. With this in mind, Laënnec rolled some papers into a tight cylinder. He placed one end on a patient's chest, above the heart, and the other end to his own ear. He could easily hear the patient's heartbeat. Laënnec had invented an early form of the stethoscope!

René Laënnec describes his experience of using a stethoscope:

> *"I was surprised and pleased to hear the beating of the heart much more clearly than if I had applied my ear directly to the chest."*

— René Laënnec, 1816

Laënnec then devised a stethoscope using a wooden tube. Like the paper model, this device was basic. It was mass-produced and sold so that doctors everywhere could try this new method of listening to a patient's heart.

The early devices were designed for doctors to listen with one ear. Later stethoscopes included an earpiece for both ears. This was called **binaural** design.

Stethoscopes have been made with many different materials, such as wood, ivory, steel, brass, chrome, and plastic.

In the early 1850s, George Cammann innovated a new model of stethoscope. He replaced some of the metal parts in the devices of that time with rubber and cotton. This change made the stethoscope more comfortable to use. His design was also binaural.

Modern stethoscopes have changed very little in their design and materials. Doctors use stethoscopes to listen to the heart and lungs. This device helps them to detect abnormalities in the heart and congestion in the lungs.

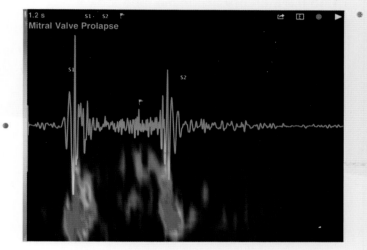

↑ In 2010, Peter Bentley, a medical researcher, invented an app that can replace a traditional stethoscope. Doctors can now use their tablets and smartphones to assess patients' heartbeats!

Peter Bentley speaks about the power of smartphones:

"Smartphones are incredibly powerful devices packed full of sensors, cameras, high-quality microphones with amazing displays. They are capable of saving lives, saving money and improving healthcare in a dramatic fashion — and we carry these massively powerful computers in our pockets."

— Peter Bentley, 2010

Thermometer

Thomas Clifford Allbutt (1836–1925) was an English doctor who invented medical thermometers. His first model included a heavy, 12-inch (30 cm) tube, and the **mercury** inside the tube took 20 minutes to display a reading of a patient's body temperature. Later models were lightweight, just six inches (15 cm) long, and registered body temperature readings in just five minutes.

Allbutt's smaller clinical thermometer was ideal for medical use. It could be used under the tongue, in the rectum, or in the armpit.

Ear Thermometer

German-born American Theodore Hannes Benzinger (1905–1999) invented the ear thermometer in 1964. His device gave a precise reading of brain temperature because the ear canal is close to the brain and they share blood vessels.

Benzinger's device paved the way for more refinements, including an **infrared** ear thermometer. Thermometer apps are now available for smartphones, too.

↓ Thomas Allbutt's clinical thermometer was popular, and remained virtually unchanged for more than 100 years.

DᴿCLIFFORD ALLBUTT'S SHORT CLIN
(SELF REGISTERI
To Set the Index before taking an observation it is best to press

90   5   100

Blood Pressure Devices

In 1773, Stephen Hales (1677–1761) was the first to measure blood pressure. The technique was quite **invasive**. Hales used a horse for his first test. He inserted a very narrow hollow pipe into an artery in the neck of the horse. The pipe was connected to a glass tube. Blood flowed into the tube and rose high inside of it. Hales could then measure the height of the blood in the tube. He called this device a manometer.

Jean Léonard Marie Poiseuille (1797–1869), a French doctor, made some improvements upon Hales's device in 1828. Instead of a glass tube, he fitted the device with a U-shaped tube, which he filled with mercury. Marks on the tube showed measurements to record the blood pressure.

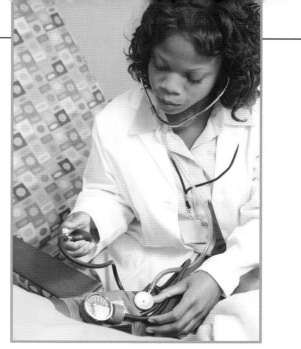

↑ A doctor measures a patient's blood pressure. Blood exerts pressure on the walls of arteries as it is pumped through the body.

The sphygmomanometer was invented by German doctor Samuel Siegfried von Basch (1837–1905) in 1881. It was the first device that did not break skin to measure blood pressure. A few years later, another improvement hit the market and became the standard device, which is still used today. The brain behind this innovation was an Italian doctor named Scipione Riva-Rocci (1863–1937).

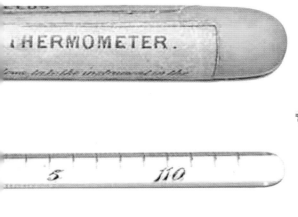

In 1704, in Cambridge, England, Stephen Hales rubbed shoulders with one of the greatest scientists in history: Isaac Newton (1642–1727). Hales was greatly influenced by Newton's ideas.

CHAPTER THREE

X-rays and Radiation Technologies

X-ray machines are used to take pictures that help health care professionals see if a bone is broken. Unfortunately, X-rays are a form of **radiation**, and too much radiation can be dangerous to people. In some situations, patients receive radiation treatments to kill harmful cells in the body, such as cancer. Used properly, radiation technologies can be effective tools for health care.

↑ This Crookes tube is much like the one that William Crookes used to observe cathode rays. Wilhelm Röntgen used this type of tube to discover X-rays.

X-rays

British chemist William Crookes (1832–1919) invented the Crookes tube in about 1875. This was a sealed glass tube that had most of the air sucked out of it, creating a near **vacuum**. Crookes was able to use such tubes to observe the properties of cathode rays—streams of **electrons**—under different conditions. While Crookes tubes are not directly related to medicine, they were used to make another important medical discovery: X-rays.

Wilhelm Conrad Röntgen (1845–1923) spent decades using Crookes tubes to study electricity. One day—completely by accident—he discovered a special type of light wave. In 1895, Röntgen was experimenting with a Crookes tube, which he'd filled with a gas. He sent an **electrostatic** charge through the tube to produce a brilliant glow. He covered the tube with black paper, which prevented visible light and **ultraviolet** light from escaping.

When a fluorescent green glowing image appeared on a **photographic plate** across the room, he knew something was different. Cathode rays could only travel about three inches (8 cm) in air. Röntgen's unique light rays traveled farther. They could pass through the thick paper, through the air, and leave a shadowy impression on a photographic plate.

Röntgen ran a series of experiments and discovered that different kinds of objects placed in front of the light produced different results on the photographic plate, depending on their **composition**. He even placed his wife's hand in front of the device. Röntgen called this unique form of light X-rays.

By the late 1800s, doctors were using X-rays to **diagnose** broken bones and find pieces of bullets inside patients. By giving us a look inside the human body, without drawing blood, X-rays revolutionized the field of medicine.

→ *The first X-ray ever produced was an image of Mrs. Röntgen's hand. The result was chilling.*

X-rays not only show human bone, but they also show metal. The X-ray of Mrs. Röntgen's hand shows a metal ring on her finger.

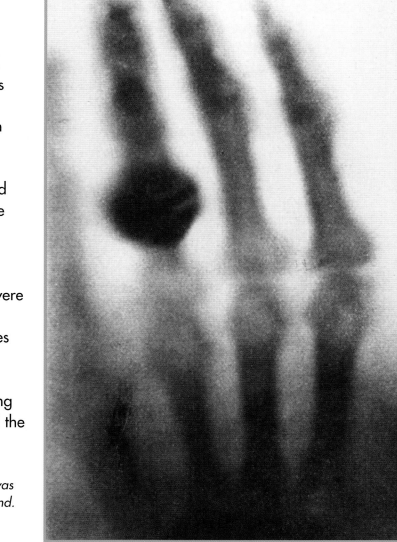

Marie Curie: The Discovery of Radium

Maria Sklodowska was born in Warsaw, Poland in 1867. Her mother was the head-mistress of a school and her father was a math and physics teacher. Maria was most like her father. She had a great passion for physics and math and a keen intellect. As a young adult, Maria moved to Paris to study science at a university called the Sorbonne. At that time, opportunities for women were limited and few women studied science. In fact, there was just one other female student in her program.

Maria changed her name to "Marie" to sound more French. In 1895, she married scientist Pierre Curie and she became known as Marie Curie. The couple worked together as scientists, and in 1898, Pierre and Marie discovered a new **radioactive** element. They named it polonium, after Marie's beloved Poland. Then they discovered another radioactive **element** called radium. Over the next few years, Marie and her fellow researchers discovered that radium kills diseased cells.

↓ *These are pages from Marie Curie's lab notebook. She was the first woman ever to win the Nobel Prize in Physics.*

Discovery of Radioactivity

In 1903, the husband-and-wife team were awarded the Nobel Prize in Physics for discovering the principles of radioactivity. The Curies were unable to attend the award ceremony due to poor health. They were suffering from long-term exposure to radiation due to their research. But Marie was determined to continue her work. She carried on, in spite of the health risks, in the hope of discovering ways to use radiation to treat health issues.

→ *Marie Curie was honored with a second Nobel Prize in 1911. This time it was in chemistry. Marie, who was now a widow, attended this ceremony to receive her award in person.*

Marie Curie believed in the importance of pure scientific research. She felt that today's research discovery could lead to tomorrow's next big medical invention:

"We must not forget that when radium was discovered no one knew that it would prove useful in hospitals. The work was one of pure science. And this is a proof that scientific work must not be considered from the point of view of the direct usefulness of it. It must be done for itself, for the beauty of science, and then there is always the chance that a scientific discovery may become, like the radium, a benefit for mankind."

— Marie Curie, 1921

Dangers of Radiation

The Curies suffered from illness due to long-term radiation exposure from handling radium. After the Curies discovered radium in 1898, people became excited about the potential health benefits of this element—and they also became ill. A radium craze took root in the 1920s. People sought out the "healthy glow" they thought radium-infused water and products would bring. They purchased devices containing radium, such as uranium blankets and water coolers lined in radioactive materials. But rather than boost their health, many of these health treatments turned out to be deadly.

Shoe-Fitting Fluoroscope

The radiation from X-rays also had negative health impacts. For example, many shoe stores in the 1930s, '40s, and '50s featured a "shoe-fitting fluoroscope." This was an X-ray device invented in 1924. Customers used the fluoroscope to check the fit of new shoes. After repeated use, however, there were cases of burned feet. Today, X-rays must be administered by health care professionals and the patient must wear a protective lead apron that shields major organs and reduces exposure.

→ *The fluoroscope was an invention that used X-rays to check the fit of shoes on people's feet. People put their feet in an opening at the bottom of the device. They looked through the metal viewing tubes at the top. This gave them an X-ray view of their feet in the shoes.*

→ Radiotherapy can be used to treat many different types of cancers.

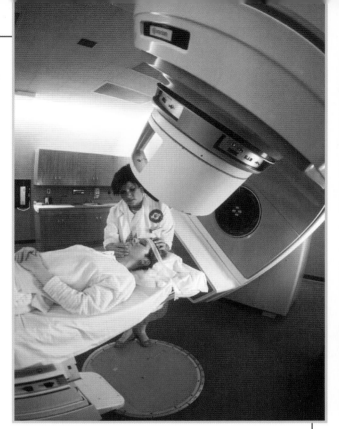

Cancer Treatment

Radium

In the past, there was one area in which the radiation from radium provided health benefits: cancer treatment. Radium radiation killed cancer cells at a faster rate than it killed normal, healthy cells. In this way, radium saved lives. Today, other sources of radiation have replaced radium for cancer treatment.

Radiotherapy

Radiotherapy, or radiation therapy, is a treatment that uses high energy X-ray beams to treat cancer patients. Doctors have been using this treatment for close to a hundred years. In some cases, radiotherapy can rid patients of cancer and also offer pain relief. Beams of radiation target cancerous tumors. The radiation kills cancer cells. It can also kill normal cells, so doctors must plan this therapy carefully. Health care professionals give patients low doses of radiation repeatedly over many days. Receiving radiation therapy is much like having a regular X-ray. Usually patients don't feel any pain during the treatment.

When the only other option is surgery, radiation can provide a less invasive treatment with a shorter recovery period, and little risk of infection. Radiation treatments can be more effective for certain types of cancer, including throat, breast, and prostate.

In the 1920s, many doctors contracted leukemia—cancer of the blood—from exposure to radiation while treating patients.

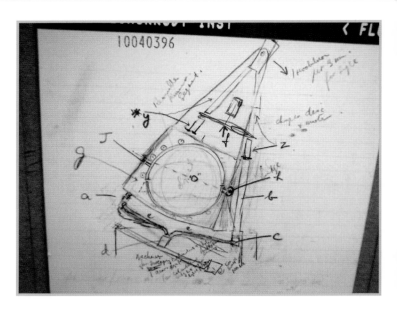

→ *This is Godfrey Hounsfield's original sketch of his proposed CT scanner device. From an early age, he was interested in electrical and mechanical devices.*

CT Scans

Computed tomography (CT) imaging changes X-rays into high-resolution video images. CT scans capture images in "slices" from several angles. CT scans produce a realistic, 3-D picture of lungs, other internal organs, or cancerous tumors. CT scans provide finer detail than flat X-rays and are much better at revealing abnormal tissues.

British electrical engineer Godfrey Newbold Hounsfield (1919–2004) invented CT technology. He was out for a walk in the country in 1967 and thought that it might be possible "to determine what was in a box by taking readings at all angles through it." He thought this approach should be possible if he used accurately aligned X-ray beams. By "readings," he meant X-ray photos.

In Hounsfield's first test, it took nine days to collect the images he needed. It took another 2.5 hours to piece together the 3-D picture on a huge computer. In 1971, Hounsfield successfully scanned a patient's brain and located a tumor. This was a huge breakthrough in medicine. CT scans became commonplace in large hospitals by 1980.

Nuclear physicist Allan Cormack (1924–1998) also invented CT technology, but he worked independently from Hounsfield. Cormack grew up in South Africa and later settled in the United States. He became intrigued by the idea of CT scans in 1956. From 1963 to 1964, Cormack published papers about his CT research. His work may have been too far ahead of its time.

It was not talked about much at all—that is, not until Hounsfield later published similar results. In 1979, Cormack and Hounsfield were honored together with a Nobel Prize in Physiology or Medicine for their pioneering work in the development of CT scans.

Magnetic Resonance Imaging (MRI) was invented in 1973. Unlike CT scans, MRI scans use radio waves to collect the cross-sectional pictures of soft tissue. After a number of these "slices," or photos, are taken, the result is similar to a CT scan: a 3-D view of what's happening inside the body.

Godfrey Hounsfield poses beside a CT scanner. The mathematics behind his invention is described as "phenomenal."

CHAPTER FOUR

Medicines

Runny nose? Cough? Headache? You may feel better after a dose of medicine. During cold and flu season, many people rely on medicines to ease their symptoms. Every year, new medicines appear on drugstore shelves. Many plant-based medicines have been around for a long time.

Aspirin: The Oldest Drug in the World

Long ago, aboriginal peoples discovered that willow bark was a good medicine to relieve pain, aches, and fevers. Ancient Greek physicians, around 400 BCE, also described the benefits of chewing willow leaves to relieve pain. Some scholars believe the ancient Greeks may have used a powdered form of the bark as well.

Chemists working in Europe in the 1820s extracted the active chemical salicin from willow bark. This was the ingredient that provided the pain relief. Salicin tasted bitter and was in the form of long, narrow crystals shaped like needles. Shortly after, Carl Jacob Löwig (1803–1890) discovered that salicylic acid occurs in a plant called meadowsweet. Salicylic acid also contains the pain-killing chemical salicin. While salicylic acid reduced pain, it also upset the stomach. Then, in 1853, Charles Frédéric Gerhardt (1816–1856) created a new compound called acetylsalicylic acid (ASA) in a lab.

↓ *People have used willow bark to treat pain and fevers for thousands of years.*

ASA was quite an innovation because it was easier on the stomach. However, the process to make ASA was difficult. Gerhardt stopped working on this project. The healing powers of ASA had not yet reached the wider public. But that would soon change with the development of the drug known as aspirin.

Medicines that reduce pain are called painkillers or analgesics.

Felix Hoffmann
Building on the Work of Charles Gerhardt

Felix Hoffmann was born in Ludwigsburg, Germany, in 1868. After university, he took up a position as a chemist in the lab at Friedrich Bayer and Company. It was there that he developed—quite by accident—a better formula for ASA. This innovation was done with help from co-worker Arthur Eichengruen. It was a much more stable and pure form of ASA than Gerhardt's earlier version. Like Gerhardt's drug, Hoffman's ASA was easy on the stomach. It reduced pain, lowered fevers, and eased inflammation in sore joints.

In 1899, Friedrich Bayer and Company marketed Hoffman's ASA as "aspirin." The drug was sold as a powder. In 1915, aspirin was produced as white tablets, much like those available today.

Aspirin was enormously popular as a treatment, but Hoffmann did not seek attention. He lived out his retirement quietly in Switzerland until his death in 1946.

↑ *Felix Hoffmann, pictured here, along with co-worker Arthur Eichengruen, developed the drug known as aspirin. Soon after, the medicine became widely known as a cure-all.*

How to Treat Diabetes?

People with diabetes have high blood glucose (sugar) because their body does not make insulin or does not use insulin correctly. People have known the symptoms of diabetes for thousands of years. In ancient times, doctors gave herbs to patients with diabetes. These medicines brought little relief. Later, American doctor Frederick Allen (1879–1964) put his diabetic patients on low-calorie diets to help manage their symptoms. Allen suggested that they eat very few **carbohydrates** or starches, such as bread, pasta, and potatoes. The diet reduced sugar in the bodies of diabetic patients, but it didn't increase their life expectancy, or how long they lived. By the late 1800s, doctors knew that the pancreas made a substance (insulin) that helped to control blood sugar. How could this knowledge help to treat people with diabetes?

Frederick Banting: The Discovery of Insulin

Everything changed with doctor Frederick Banting (1891–1941) and his assistant doctor Charles Best (1899–1978). These two researchers discovered insulin and the role it plays in the body in 1922. Banting wanted to find a way to extract insulin from the pancreas, the organ where insulin is produced. He was intrigued by an article he had read about the pancreatic duct. It gave Banting an idea he was eager to test. He approached John J. R. Macleod, a professor of physiology at the University of Toronto. Macleod agreed to let Banting use his lab. Banting appointed Charles Best as his assistant.

↑ Born in Alliston, Ontario, Canada, Frederick Banting went to the University of Toronto where he earned a medical degree. He served during World War I.

Over the course of the summer the two made history. Their discovery of insulin made life easier for millions of people with diabetes.

Since that time, most people with diabetes have been able to live fairly normal lives. They can give themselves insulin injections to keep their glucose levels stable. Today, thanks to insulin, most people with diabetes can enjoy long, healthy lives. It is still important for people with diabetes—and everyone else—to plan healthy meals and snacks, to never skip meals, and to exercise regularly.

In the 1600s, doctor Thomas Willis (1621–1675) of London, England, used a urine taste test. This test was used to diagnose patients with "honeyed" diabetes.

↑ *This is a page from Banting and Best's lab notebook from 1921, while they worked on the discovery of insulin.*

Upon receiving a Nobel Prize in Medicine, Banting delivered this message at the awards ceremony:

"With the relief of the symptoms of this disease, and with the increased strength and vigor resulting from the increased diet, the pessimistic, melancholy diabetic becomes optimistic and cheerful. Insulin is not a cure for diabetes; it is a treatment."

— Frederick Banting, 1923

Penicillin

Over 3000 years ago, doctors in China applied moldy tofu to infected cuts. Antibiotic substances in the mold killed infections and helped wounds heal. In parts of Europe, people used moldy bread to treat infections.

In 1874, British scientist and doctor William Roberts (1830–1899) observed that some types of fungi stopped growing when bacteria were introduced. Then, French scientist Louis Pasteur noticed that bacteria stopped growing when they were tainted with penicillium fungus.

In 1928, Alexander Fleming (1881–1955) was doing experiments with another bacterium. He was careless in his lab work and left the covers off his samples. This led to contamination with mold. The contamination made a substance that killed the bacteria. Fleming isolated the substance in the mold and called it "penicillin." This was a breakthrough discovery! Fleming had found the world's first **antibiotic** drug. In time, penicillin revolutionized medicine.

In 1938, Howard Florey (1898–1968) and Ernst Chain (1906–1979), two scientists working in England, checked Fleming's results. They did many tests and came up with a method to further purify the penicillin.

Next, they developed a technique for large-scale production of this drug. They joined with American drug companies and penicillin became a "wonder drug." It was used all over the world.

Soldiers were among the first people to be treated with penicillin.

Dorothy Crowfoot Hodgkin

Dorothy Hodgkin (1910–1994) became interested in chemistry and crystals at age 10. She focused her studies on X-ray crystallography and was at the top of her field by the age of 30.

Hodgkin then made an important finding toward the discovery of penicillin. Using X-ray crystallography, she showed the arrangement and structure of atoms in penicillin. However, Chain, Florey, and Fleming alone were honored with a Nobel Prize in 1945 for the discovery of penicillin. At that time, Chain explained Hodgkin's important role in the discovery: "The final solution of the problem of the structure of penicillin came from crystallographic X-ray studies." That had been Hodgkin's work.

Dorothy Crowfoot Hodgkin made an important contribution to the discovery of penicillin. Hodgkin went on to determine the structure of many medicines and substances, including insulin.

In 1964, she was awarded the Nobel Prize for Chemistry. This was a testament to her great contributions to medical science.

This quote comes from Hodgkin's 1964 Nobel lecture:

"A great advantage of X-ray analysis as a method of chemical structure analysis is its power to show some totally unexpected and surprising structure with, at the same time, complete certainty."

— Dorothy Crowfoot Hodgkin, 1964

CHAPTER FIVE

Genetics

→ *This is the famous "Photo 51" taken by Rosalind Franklin. It is an image of DNA. Experts could tell by this picture that DNA was in the shape of a helix. And later they realized that DNA was in the shape of a double helix. See the double-helix shape of DNA on page 36 of this book.*

Look at pictures of your family members. What looks the same or different? Chances are you share some characteristics with your family. Genetics is a field that studies the passing on—or inheritance—of traits from parents to children. Some medical conditions can be inherited from our parents and grandparents. Learning about genetics can help doctors develop treatments.

Solving the DNA Puzzle

In 1868, Swiss biologist Friedrich Miescher (1844 –1895) used a microscope to look at the **nuclei** of living cells. He isolated what was later identified as DNA, the genetic map that defines our characteristics. Miescher called the substance nuclein. He and his colleagues thought there might be a link between nuclein and information about inherited traits. However, they couldn't prove it.

Miescher collected soiled bandages to do his work. He scraped the pus off of the bandages to obtain a supply of white blood cells. He observed the nuclei of these living cells. Today, with our high standards for sanitation and our knowledge of the spread of germs, this practice would not be accepted.

In 1943, researchers Oswald Avery, Colin MacLeod, and Maclyn McCarty found evidence that DNA carries all the genetic material for each individual. Their conclusion paved the way for future work on the passing of traits from parents to offspring.

Rosalind Franklin: The Structure of DNA

As a high school student in London, England, Rosalind Franklin (1920 – 1958) excelled in science. At this time, many men thought women should stay at home and not pursue careers. But Franklin wanted to study science at university. She went to study at the University of Cambridge and became a scientist.

Franklin used X-rays to photograph a crystal of deoxyribonucleic acid—DNA. After observing some spectacular results, she sought out scientist Dorothy Hodgkin. Together, they studied the images of DNA and pondered the possibilities. Franklin's work on this set of images revealed that the structure of DNA was that of a **helix**.

→ *Rosalind Franklin was a top-notch scientist whose work made a significant contribution to unraveling the puzzle of DNA.*

Francis Crick (1916 – 2004) and James Watson (1928 –) used Franklin's data—without her knowledge—in the hypothesis they formed in 1953. Franklin's results helped Watson and Crick discover that the structure of DNA was not a single helix, but a double helix. Franklin came to the same conclusion, but Watson and Crick's findings were published first. Watson and Crick received all the credit for this discovery for many years. They also received a Nobel Prize in 1962.

"Science and everyday life cannot and should not be separated."

— Rosalind Franklin, 1940

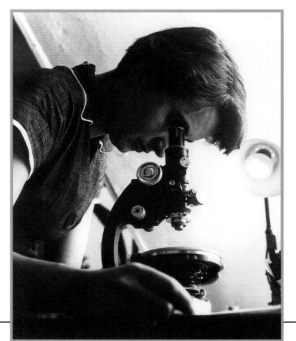

The Genetic Code

The year 1966 marked the cracking of the genetic code: the discovery of the coding for all 20 **amino acids** that make up protein. Then, in 1969, James Shapiro, Jonathan Beckwith, and their team isolated a single gene for the first time. **Genes** carry information about physical traits, like whether a person has blue or brown eyes. Some genes carry information that cause disease. As scientists isolated, or "mapped," other genes, the genetic makeup of humans became better understood. Genetic maps have proved useful in learning more about genetic disorders.

↓ *This picture illustrates the double-helix shape of DNA. There are 25,000 to 35,000 genes in the DNA of each human cell.*

Genes That Cause Disease

The first disease gene that was mapped was for Huntington's disease. It is a neurological disease that causes people to lose control of their muscles. The American neuropsychologist Nancy Wexler (1945 –) and her research team did this work in 1983. (Wexler is often called "the gene hunter.") Ten years later, in 1993, they located the faulty gene sequence for Huntington's on a particular **chromosome**. Wexler hopes that genetic research will eventually lead to a cure for this deadly disease.

Scientists discovered the faulty gene that causes **cystic fibrosis** in 1985. The gene for **muscular dystrophy** was found in 1986.

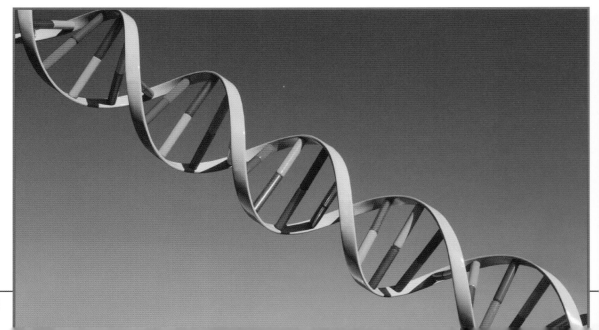

Two faulty genes that can lead to breast cancer were discovered in 1994 and 1995. Women who carry these genes are at higher risk of developing breast cancer.

The isolation of particular genes has led to improvements in treatments for diseases. The more we know about human genes, the better equipped we are to improve human health. It's an exciting time in the field of genetics!

Mapping the human **genome**—or the Human Genome Project—involved researchers from all over the world. It began in 1990 and was completed in 2003.

Barbara McClintock

Barbara McClintock (1902–1992) was drawn to science as a young child in Hartford, Connecticut. She asked lots of questions and sought out information. After studying botany, she focused her research on genes. McClintock began her experiments on corn in 1944. In 1950, she announced her theory that genes could "jump" to new locations on a chromosome. Her peers at the National Academy of Sciences didn't take her seriously. "They thought I was crazy, absolutely mad," she recalled. Others confirmed her theory in the 1970s and 1980s.

↑ Barbara McClintock observed different patterns of color in corn. This led to her theory that genes could move along chromosomes like a dragonfly flitting from one flower to another.

McClintock's discovery advanced the field of genetics. It enabled scientists and medical researchers to improve health treatments for people. In 1983, McClintock received a Nobel Prize in Physiology or Medicine for her extraordinary discovery.

CHAPTER SIX

Prosthetics

People who are missing an arm or leg use artificial limbs to walk, dance, run, reach, grasp, eat, and play. Artificial devices that resemble parts of the human body are called prosthetics.

There are stories of artificial limbs that go back to ancient cultures. For example, ancient Greek historian Herodotus recorded an incredible story: a runaway prisoner escaped by cutting off his own foot. Then, the escapee found a wooden limb to help him walk. This is the first written record of an artificial leg. In another case, researchers in Egypt found a prosthetic device that was used to replace a missing big toe. It is estimated to be close to 3000 years old. It is made of leather and carved wood. In 1858, archaeologists digging in Capri, Italy, unearthed an artificial leg made of copper and wood. Experts believe the false leg is from 300 BCE.

Ambroise Paré (1510–1590), an early surgeon from sixteenth century France, treated injured soldiers. These soldiers often lost limbs in battle. Paré was determined to care for soldiers who survived such a debilitating injury—and

↑ Paré included hand-drawn pictures of his inventions in his books about medicinal treatments. This is one of his pictures: an artificial hand.

didn't die from infection. He invented artificial limbs or prosthetic devices for these men. The prosthetics assisted the patient with basic tasks and everyday life. This helped soldiers to carry on with their lives normally, rather than being confined to a bed or wheelchair.

Better Prosthetics
Building on the work of Paré

Paré's inventions were much-celebrated. Since his time, prosthetics have improved greatly. For example, the rubber hand was invented in 1863. It was much more realistic than previous models. The fingers were made of soft rubber.

Later, World War I and World War II resulted in an increase in amputees—people who had lost limbs. A special sock was invented for above-knee prosthesis. This helped amputees to enjoy more comfort and stability. Next came stronger and more lightweight materials, such as carbon fiber, which was first developed for the aircraft industry. Inventors also borrowed technology from the computer world to create a state-of-the-art design program for developing realistic skin using silicone.

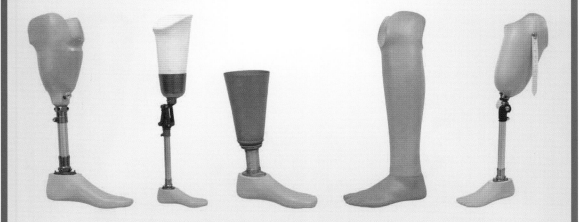

↑ *Many types of prosthetic legs have been invented in the past century. They are made of modern, lightweight materials.*

"The art of medicine is to cure sometimes, to relieve often, to comfort always."

— Ambroise Paré, 16th century

Superhuman Devices

A waterskiing accident led to the loss of Van Phillips's (1954 –) lower leg. This 21-year-old American athlete was determined to keep active. In fact, Phillips wanted to learn to run again. He just needed a device to replace his lost foot.

After earning a degree in biomedical engineering, Phillips began his career as a biomedical engineer—someone who designs devices, such as artificial limbs, for use in health care. In 1981, he made a prototype for a foot, inspired by the C-shaped foot of a cheetah. After trying it himself, he quit his regular job and focused on refining his device. By 1984, he began manufacturing his prosthetic feet for Paralympic sprinters and running enthusiasts.

↓ *Van Phillips created the first Cheetah foot, made of carbon graphite and designed to flex and spring. American athlete Aimee Mullins wears these prosthetic feet to compete in the long jump.*

→ *This Flex-Foot is similar to the Cheetah foot designed by Van Phillips.*

Van Phillips wasn't happy with the prosthetics available for amputees like himself. The innovator explained what it was like when he first received a prosthetic foot:

"Feet in those days were often made of balsa wood. Light, but with no flexibility and no method of storing energy."

— Van Phillips, 2010

Robotic Arm

Lead investigator Michael McLoughlin and his team of biomedical engineers have invented a sophisticated robotic arm. Users of this device use their brain to work the device. Surgeons embed a sensor in the brain of the user. This sensor activates a connection between the brain and the device. In this way, the user can move the prosthetic arm as if it were a part of their body. The user of the device can even grasp small objects, just by thinking about what he or she would like to do. This very closely imitates what able-bodied people do every time they move or manipulate their arms. What a great innovation in prosthetics!

Beyond Prosthetics

French neuroscientist Grégoire Courtine (1975 –) has a PhD in Experimental Medicine. He has been working as a bioengineer since 2004. His current research focuses on spinal cord injury and developing technology to help retrain the brain to achieve body movement. Courtine has made advances in restoring spinal cord function, bringing affected individuals closer to walking.

Courtine foresees a time of incredible advances to help people with different physical needs:

"We're entering a really exciting area where we can develop all sorts of very complicated technologies that can actually have biomedical applications and improve the quality of life for people. It's a revolution."

— Grégoire Courtine, 2012

CONCLUSION

Some think the future of medicine will feature even more inventive technologies than we have seen in the past. Already, electronic devices check vital signs and give prescriptions for medicine. Since the early 2000s, it has been possible for surgeons in one location to operate on patients who are in another community. Surgeons do these operations using robotic devices. What inventions could be next?

↓ *This surgeon controls a robotic device to perform an operation on a patient in another location. This type of surgery is known as remote surgery. Remote surgery is performed on patients in war zones, small mountain villages, or other hard-to-reach areas of the world.*

Many benefits come with these new medical technologies, but the role of people is critical, too. Warm interactions with caring friends, family, and medical staff are a vital part of recovery.

Medical advances continue to build on past inventions, innovations, and discoveries. Health care workers are always renewing their training to use these new devices, medicines, and technologies. And inventions that today serve one purpose may in the future be hugely advantageous in ways we haven't yet dreamed up. As we move toward a bright future, we can expect to take great strides in medicine.

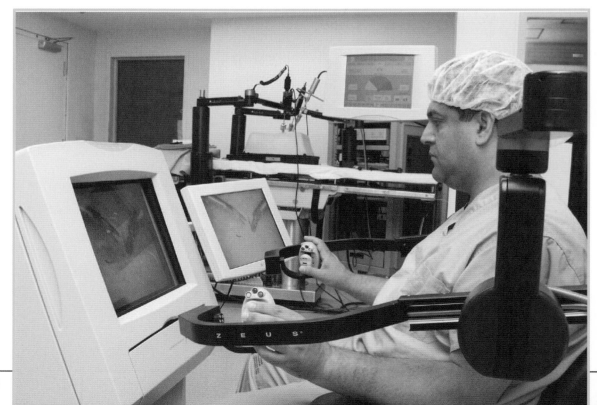

Learning More

Books

Becker, Helaine. *What's the Big Idea? Inventions that Changed Life on Earth Forever.* Maple Tree Press, 2009.

Di Domenico, Kelly. *Super Women in Science* (The Women's Hall of Fame Series). Second Story Press, 2002.

Editors of YES Mag. *Robots: From Everyday to Out of This World.* Kids Can Press, 2008.

Lee, Dora. *Biomimicry: Inventions Inspired by Nature.* Kids Can Press, 2011.

Websites

Ancient Chinese Medicine
http://www.historyforkids.org/learn/china/science/chinamedicine.htm
This encyclopedia-style article includes links to terms such as "yin," "yang," and "smallpox."

Ancient Egypt: Inventions and Technology
http://www.ducksters.com/history/ancient_egypt/inventions_and_technology.php
The text on this website is organized under subheadings, such as "Writing," "Medicine," and "Mathematics," and "Fun Facts about the Inventions of Ancient Egypt."

"Thought-powered bionic arm 'like something from space'"
http://www.cnn.com/2013/05/02/tech/innovation/bionic-robotic-arm-limb-amputee/index.html
The Art of Movement is a CNN show that looks at innovations in science, technology, and other fields. This episode shows a prototype for Michael McLoughlin's team's robotic arm, poised to revolutionize the future of prosthetics.

History of Medicine
http://www.knowitall.org/kidswork/hospital/history/index.html
Click key points on a timeline to reveal webpages that describe different ages in the history of medicine, from ancient times to modern medicine.

Timeline

900 Egyptian surgeon Ammar ibn Ali al-Mawsili uses syringe-like device.

1066 Vikings from Norway invade England in The Norman Conquest.

1348–1350 The Black Death kills up to 200 million people in Europe.

1505 Leonardo da Vinci paints the Mona Lisa.

1773 Stephen Hales measures a horse's blood pressure.

1776 The United States declares independence as a nation.

1789–1799 Peasants revolt against the monarchy in The French Revolution.

1796 Edward Jenner invents the first vaccine.

1812–1815 The United States and Great Britain engage in war in North America.

1816 René Laënnec invents the stethoscope.

1840s Ignaz Semmelweis instructs health care workers to wash their hands and disinfect.

1853 Alexander Wood invents the hypodermic syringe.

1853–1856 Florence Nightingale promotes hand washing, thereby saving many lives.

1862 Louis Pasteur invented the process of pasteurization, killing harmful bacteria.

1865 Joseph Lister begins to use carbolic acid as a disinfectant during surgery.

1866 Thomas Clifford Allbutt invents the first compact clinical thermometer.

1867 Canada becomes a country.

1868 Friedrich Miescher observes the nuclei of living cells, which he calls nuclein. It is later identified as DNA.

1875 William Crookes invents the Crookes tube, a precursor to modern X-ray technology.

1876 Samuel Siegfried von Basch invents the sphygmomanometer.

1895 Wilhelm Conrad Röntgen discovers X-rays.

1898 Marie Curie and Pierre Curie discover radium—believed to have health benefits.

1899 Felix Hoffmann invents aspirin.

1900 Jules Bordet discovers the bacterium that causes whooping cough.

1914–1918 More than 9 million soldiers die in World War I, or the Great War.

1922 Frederick Banting and Charles Best discover insulin.

1928 Alexander Fleming discovers penicillin.

1939–1945 More than 50 million people die in World War II.

1950 Barbara McClintock announces genes can jump to new locations on chromosomes.

1953 Watson and Crick discover the structure of DNA with help from Rosalind Franklin.

1956 Colin Murdoch invents the disposable syringe.

1969 Neil Armstrong walks on the Moon.

James Shapiro and Jonathan Beckwith isolate the first gene.

1972 Godfrey Newbold Hounsfield invents CT scanning technology.

1981–1984 Van Phillips invents a flexible prosthetic device called the Cheetah foot.

1982 Insulin is made using human DNA inserted into bacteria.

1983–1993 Nancy Wexler maps the Huntington's disease gene and locates its exact location on a chromosome.

1993 World Wide Web available for use by the general public.

2003 The human genome is sequenced.

2013 Biomedical engineer Michael McLoughlin invents a robotic arm and hand controlled by the brain.

Glossary

amino acids An organic acid needed to build proteins and sustain life; some of these cannot be made in the body and must be provided in the foods we eat.

antibiotic A medicine that kills the bacteria that cause infection without harming other cells in the body

autopsies Examinations made to find the cause of death

bacteria One-celled organisms that may be harmful or beneficial to humans

balms Healing ointments that are often made from sticky substances (resins) from trees and shrubs

binaural Having two earpieces

biohazardous A biological substance or condition that can be harmful to health

calcium chloride A white crystalline compound that is used as a drying agent

carbohydrate A food component that provides energy

chromosome Structure found within cells that carries genetic material; humans normally have 23 pairs of chromosomes

circulation Movement of blood through the heart, veins, and arteries

composition The way something is put together; the order or structure of things

cystic fibrosis A fatal, inherited disease that creates a build-up of mucus in the lungs and digestive organs

diagnose To identify the nature of a health issue by examining the symptoms

disinfectant Something that kills germs

electrons Very small particles that are part of an atom that move around the nucleus of an atom and have a negative charge

electrostatic Relating to static electricity

element One of the simple substances in the universe that cannot be broken down into another substance (e.g., oxygen is an element, but water is not, because water can be broken down into oxygen and hydrogen)

genes Segments of DNA that are responsible for inherited characteristics; basic unit of heredity found on chromosomes

genome The complete set of genetic material for an organism

helix A coiled object; the double-helix of DNA is like a curved or spiral ladder

hypothesized To make an informed guess

immunity The ability to resist catching an infectious disease upon contact

infection Invasion of microorganisms (e.g., bacteria) into a wound or body part, which often leads to pus, swelling, and toxicity

inflammation Swelling

infrared An invisible electromagnetic radiation that has a longer wavelength than the red wavelengths we can see

inoculation The process of having a substance injected into a person or animal to help them develop an immunity against a disease, such as smallpox

insulin A substance that helps to regulate sugar in the blood

invasive Introducing a medical instrument into a body

lesions Infected or diseased patches of skin or other body tissues

mercury A heavy, silver-white metal that is one of the chemical elements; it is liquid at room temperature; used in thermometers and barometers

muscular dystrophy An inherited disease in which muscles become smaller and weaker over time

nuclei The plural form of nucleus, which is the central part of an atom

pasteurization The process of heating a substance for a certain length of time to kill harmful bacteria

photographic plate An object used in early forms of photography on which the image would appear

radiation Waves of energy sent out by radioactive material

radioactive An element that gives off energy in the form of particles or rays

salves Substances used to heal wounds or make them feel better

sanitation The promotion of hygiene and prevention of disease by keeping conditions clean

smallpox A serious disease caused by the variola virus, which is highly contagious and leaves scars

solutions Liquid mixtures in which two or more substances are combined

sterilized When something is cleaned using an antiseptic substance or process (e.g., heat) to kill harmful bacteria

symptoms Indicators of a health condition, disease, or illness that a patient may report to a doctor

ultraviolet Light that is beyond the violet end of the spectrum of visible light with a wavelength between visible light and X-rays

vaccines Medicines taken orally or injected by syringe that help people develop immunity to specific diseases

vacuum A space or container that has had most of the air removed

whooping cough An infectious bacterial disease, characterized by coughing spasms and a distinctive "whoop" sound; also known as pertussis

Index